W0246795

THE LITTLE BOOK OF

CALM

First published in 2025 by OH
An Imprint of HEADLINE PUBLISHING GROUP LIMITED

2

Cataloguing in Publication Data is available from the British Library

ISBN 978-1-03542-252-4

Compiled and written by: Jason Ward
Editorial: Saneaah Muhammad
Designed and typeset in Dosis by: Stephen Cary
Project manager: Russell Porter
Production: Rachel Burgess
Printed and bound in Dubai

MIX
Paper | Supporting responsible forestry
FSC® C104740

Headline's policy is to use papers that are natural, renewable and recyclable products and made from wood grown in well-managed forests and other controlled sources. The logging and manufacturing processes are expected to conform to the environmental regulations of the country of origin.

HEADLINE PUBLISHING GROUP LIMITED
An Hachette UK Company
Carmelite House, 50 Victoria Embankment, London EC4Y 0DZ

The authorised representative in the EEA is Hachette Ireland, 8 Castlecourt Centre, Dublin 15, D15 XTP3, Ireland (email: info@hbgi.ie)

www.headline.co.uk   www.hachette.co.uk

THE LITTLE BOOK OF
CALM

FOR WHEN LIFE
GETS A LITTLE TOUGH

CONTENTS

INTRODUCTION

How do you slow down when the world has never moved faster? How do you do nothing when there's so much to do? How do you find a moment's peace when the phone in your pocket buzzes every few minutes? Making time to recentre yourself can easily feel like just another item on your to-do list, pushed further and further back in favour of more "important" activities.

However, what if tranquillity isn't a far-off destination, but instead something you can find all around you – or, more precisely, within you? Rather than buying more products that overpromise and exaggerate their benefits, perhaps mindfulness is something that can be cultivated and refined in small, gentle ways, by paying attention to both yourself and the world around you.

Serenity isn't just a luxury, available only for other people: in a world that demands our constant attention, finding tranquillity is a vital act of self-preservation. This is a skill that can be learned, practised and refined over time. Some days it will come effortlessly, while others may test your resolve. But with each moment of mindfulness, you're forging an anchor that can hold steady in rough seas.

The Little Book of Calm is an invitation to pause, to breathe and to rediscover the quiet strength that resides inside you. It's a gentle reminder that amid the tumult of daily life, there's always a little space for calmness – an inner peace that you can access, no matter the circumstances. In these pages, you'll find wisdom from inspiring minds, whose words offer solace and guidance for nurturing calmness in your life: a collection of stepping stones, perhaps, on the journey to inner peace. Hopefully, this book will be a companion in those moments when it might be most useful.

CHAPTER
1

INNER CALM

Inner peace may occasionally seem like a reservoir; liable to drying up from overuse or during a particularly bad drought.

Perhaps it is better to think of it as a natural spring: a replenishing source of tranquillity from somewhere deep within, a draught of strength that you can draw from when you need it.

I will be calm; I will be
mistress of myself.

Jane Austen

Your mind will answer most
questions if you learn to relax
and wait for the answer.

William S. Burroughs

Breath is the power behind
all things. I breathe in and know
that good things will happen.

Tao Porchon-Lynch

Nothing can bring you
peace but yourself.

Ralph Waldo Emerson

Gentleness is strength under control. It is the ability to stay calm, no matter what happens.

Elizabeth George

Within you, there is a stillness
and a sanctuary to which you can
retreat at any time and be yourself.

Hermann Hesse

Nothing is so bitter that a calm
mind cannot find comfort in it.

Seneca the Younger

When we are unable to find tranquillity within ourselves, it is useless to seek it elsewhere.

François de La Rochefoucauld

Peace is present right here and now,
in ourselves and in everything.

Thích Nhất Hạnh

Calmness of will is a
sign of grandeur.

Johann Kaspar Lavater

The sense of being well-dressed
gives a feeling of inward tranquillity
which religion is powerless to bestow.

C. F. Forbes

First of my own personal requirements is inner calm. This, I think, is an essential. One of the secrets of using your time well is to gain a certain ability to maintain peace within yourself so that much can go on around you and you can stay calm inside.

Eleanor Roosevelt

Do not anticipate trouble or worry about what may never happen. Keep in the sunlight.

Benjamin Franklin

Going to a sensational
murder trial is the only way
I can relax.

John Waters

Calmness of mind is one of the beautiful jewels of wisdom. It is the result of long and patient effort in self-control. Its presence is an indication of ripened experience, and of a more than ordinary knowledge of the laws and operations of thought.

James Allen

In your patience ye are strong.

Elizabeth Barrett Browning

Whenever in doubt,
turn off your mind, relax,
float downstream.

Timothy Leary

Mightiest powers buy
deepest calms are fed,

And sleep, how oft, on
things that gentlest be.

Bryan Procter

Freedom is a calm mind.

Shane Parrish

Serenity of spirit and turbulence
of action – that should make up
the sum of man's life.

Vita Sackville-West

Remain calm, serene, always in command of yourself. You will then find out how easy it is to get along.

Paramahansa Yogananda

Give your stress wings
and let it fly away.

Terri Guillemets

A happy life
consists in tranquillity
of mind.

Marcus Tullius Cicero

Pride is lofty, calm,
immovable; vanity is uncertain,
capricious, and unjust.

Nicolas Chamfort

The language of excitement
is at best picturesque merely.
You must be calm before you
can utter oracles.

Henry David Thoreau

Peace goes into the making
of a poet as flour goes into
the making of bread.

Pablo Neruda

The very secret of life for me,
I believed, was to maintain in
the midst of rushing events an
inner tranquillity.

Margaret Bourke-White

It takes a snowflake two
hours to fall from cloud to earth.
Can't you just see its slow,
peaceful descent?

Amy Krouse Rosenthal

Don't try to force anything.
Let life be a deep let-go.
God opens millions of
flowers every day without
forcing their buds.

Osho

I took a deep breath and listened to the old brag of my heart: I am, I am, I am.

Sylvia Plath

CHAPTER
2

CALM
IN THE STORM

Writers and thinkers have always been drawn to imagery of rough seas and bad weather when trying to describe what it's like to be alive.

The idea has stuck because it feels precise and true: it's not just that life can be tempestuous, but that, in time, those tempests always pass.

The ship of my life may or may not be sailing on calm and amiable seas. The challenging days of my existence may or may not be bright and promising. Stormy or sunny days, glorious or lonely nights, I maintain an attitude of gratitude. If I insist on being pessimistic, there is always tomorrow. Today I am blessed.

Maya Angelou

If you are wholly perplexed
and in straits, have patience, for
patience is the key to joy.

Rumi

Nothing baffles the schemes
of evil people so much as the calm
composure of great souls.

Honoré Gabriel Riqueti, Count of Mirabeau

Worrying is like a rocking chair;
it gives you something to do,
but it gets you nowhere.

Glenn Turner

Aequam memento rebus in
arduis servare mentem.

(Remember to keep a clear head
in difficult times.).

Horace

You flounder through life,
struggling desperately so you
won't drown, even though you
would float if you'd just relax.

Natsuki Takaya

Don't feel guilty if you don't know
what you want to do with your life.
The most interesting people
I know didn't know at 22 what
they wanted to do with their lives.
Some of the most interesting
40-year-olds I know still don't.

Mary Schmich

If there be light, then there is darkness; if cold, heat; if height, depth; if solid, fluid; if hard, soft; if rough, smooth; if calm, tempest; if prosperity, adversity; if life, death.

Pythagoras

We should not try to alter circumstances but to adapt ourselves to them as they really are, just as sailors do. They don't try to change the winds or the sea but ensure that they are always ready to adapt themselves to conditions. In a flat calm they use the oars; with a following breeze they hoist full sail; in a head wind they shorten sail or heave to.

Bion of Borysthenes

If I have a clear conscience
and a calm spirit, I dare to face an
enemy of ten million.

Koichi Tohei

I have become aware
of just how fragile life is.
We walk in the sunlight,
ignoring the shadows.

Jackie Ashley

The willow submits to the wind
and prospers until one day it is
many willows – a wall against the
wind. This is the willow's purpose.

Frank Herbert

Many a calm river begins
as a turbulent waterfall,
yet none hurtles and foams
all the way to the sea.

Mikhail Lermontov

Your life will be in order
when disorder ceases to
bother you.

James Pierce

I'm full of fears and I do my best
to avoid difficulties and any kind
of complications. I like everything
around me to be clear as crystal
and completely calm.

Alfred Hitchcock

The pursuit, even of the best things,
ought to be calm and tranquil.

Marcus Tullius Cicero

Fighting the wounds of the past will only deepen those wounds. Relaxation is the method that heals the wounds of the mind, not reaction.

Mata Amritanandamayi

I pray thee, spare thyself
at times: for it becomes a
wise man sometimes to
relax the high pressure of
his attention to work.

Thomas Aquinas

For the warrior, every moment
is a challenge to be genuine, and
each challenge is delightful. When
you let go properly, you can relax
and enjoy the challenge.

Chögyam Trungpa

If after every tempest come
such calms, May the winds blow till
they have waken'd death!

William Shakespeare

The most intense conflicts, if overcome, leave behind a sense of security and calm that is not easily disturbed. It is just these intense conflicts and their conflagration which are needed to produce valuable and lasting results.

Carl Jung

Hope is like a path in the countryside: originally there was no path – yet, as people are walking all the time in the same spot, a way appears.

Lu Xun

'What makes the desert beautiful',
said the little prince,
'is that it hides, somewhere, a well.'

Antoine de Saint-Exupéry

By staying calm,
you increase
your resistance
against any
kind of storms.

Mehmet Murat ildan

How calm, how beautiful comes on
The stilly hour, when storms are gone!
When warring winds have died away,
And clouds, beneath the glancing ray,
Melt off, and leave the land and sea
Sleeping in bright tranquillity!

Thomas Moore

There was never yet philosopher
That could endure the toothache patiently.

William Shakespeare

You could not direct the wind,
but you could trim your sail
so as to propel your vessel as
you pleased, no matter which
way the wind blew.

Cora L. V. Hatch

If a man insisted always on
being serious, and never allowed
himself a bit of fun and relaxation,
he would go mad or become
unstable without knowing it.

Herodotus

I feel a certain calm. There is safety in the midst of danger. What would life be if we had no courage to attempt anything?
It will be a hard pull for me; the tide rises high, almost to the lips and perhaps higher still, how can I know? But I shall fight my battle, and sell my life dearly, and try to win and get the best of it.

Vincent van Gogh

E anche il mare,
grande che sia, si calma.

(Even the sea, great
though it be, grows calm.)

Italian proverb

CHAPTER 3

THE BEAUTY OF STILLNESS

In an odd way, we have cause to be grateful about the chaos of modern life. The busier the world gets, the more we're able to cherish the virtues of silence and stillness.

As such qualities become harder to find, we see how important they've always been, and what they bring to our lives.

Perhaps it is possible to discover
more in silence than in speech.
Or perhaps it is only that those who
are silent among us learn to listen.

Alice Hoffman

In stillness, we find our peace.
Knowing peace at home, we bring
peace into the world.

Katrina Kenison

Silence is the element in which
great things fashion themselves
together; that at length they may
emerge, full-formed and majestic,
into the daylight of Life, which they
are thenceforth to rule.

Thomas Carlyle

Before embarking on important undertakings, sit quietly, calm your senses and thoughts and meditate deeply. You will then be guided by the great creative power of Spirit.

Paramahansa Yogananda

Silence is essential. We need silence just as much as we need air, just as much as plants need light. If our minds are crowded with words and thoughts, there is no space for us.

Thích Nhất Hạnh

It is not necessary that you leave the house. Remain at your table and listen. Do not even listen, only wait. Do not even wait, be wholly still and alone. The world will present itself to you for its unmasking, it can do no other, in ecstasy it will writhe at your feet.

Franz Kafka

Take heed of still waters,
they quick pass away.

English proverb

My personal hobbies are reading,
listening to music, and silence.

Edith Sitwell

How sweet and soothing is this hour of calm! I thank thee, night! for thou has chased away these horrid bodements which, amidst the throng, I could not dissipate; and with the blessing of thy benign and quiet influence now will I to my couch, although to rest is almost wronging such a night as this.

Lord Byron

Silence is always beautiful,
and a silent person is always more
beautiful than one who talks.

Fyodor Dostoyevsky

If sleep is the apogee of physical relaxation, boredom is the apogee of mental relaxation. Boredom is the dream bird that hatches the egg of experience.

Walter Benjamin

Silence best speaks the mind.

Phineas Fletcher

Religious truth, or for that matter
any truth, requires a calm and meditative
atmosphere for its percolation.

Mahatma Gandhi

The ideal of calm
exists in a sitting cat.

Jules Renard

Go placidly amid the noise
and haste, and remember what
peace there may be in silence.

Max Ehrmann

Timely silence, then, is precious,
for it is nothing less than the mother
of the wisest thoughts.

Diadochos of Photiki

If you peel back the layers
of your life – the frenzy,
the noise – stillness is waiting.
That stillness is you.

Oprah Winfrey

A fence to wisdom is silence.

Akiba ben Joseph

The snow has quietness in it;
no songs, no smells, no shouts
or traffic. When I speak my
own voice shocks me.

Anne Sexton

What shall I say to you?
What can I say
Better than silence is?

Henry Wadsworth Longfellow

I've begun to realize that you can listen to silence and learn from it. It has a quality and dimension all its own.

Chaim Potok

For mine own part,
I could be well content

To entertain the lag-end
of my life

With quiet hours.

William Shakespeare

The sole art that suits me is
that which, rising from unrest,
tends toward serenity.

André Gide

Under all speech that is good for anything there lies a silence that is better. Silence is deep as Eternity; speech is shallow as Time.

Thomas Carlyle

Can you be still and look inside?
If so, then you know the truth is always
available, and always responsive.

Lao Tzu

There are times when silence is the best
way to yell at the top of your voice.

Orlando Aloysius Battista

Tranquillity is contagious, peace is contagious. One only thinks of the contagiousness of illness, but there is the contagion of serenity and joy.

Anaïs Nin

Existence itself does not feel horrible;
it feels like an ecstasy, rather, which we
have only to be still to experience.

John Updike

CHAPTER
4

THE RHYTHMS OF NATURE

The Scottish writer Nan Shepherd once referred to hill climbing as an appetite that grows in feeding – "Like drink and passion, it intensifies life to the point of glory."

That essential response can be drawn from visiting many wild and quiet places; sometimes it's worth just seeing where your feet take you.

On the surface of the ocean, men wage war and destroy each other; but down here, just a few feet beneath the surface, there is a calm and peace.

Jules Verne

O soft day, O calm day,
made clear for our sake!

William Morris

Mere communion with nature, mere contact with the free air, exercise a soothing yet strengthening influence on the wearied spirit, calm the storm of passion, and soften the heart when shaken by sorrow to its inmost depths.

Johann Wolfgang von Goethe

It is all very beautiful and magical here – a quality which cannot be described. You have to live it and breathe it, let the sun bake into you.

Ansel Adams

In the woods, we return to reason and faith. There I feel that nothing can befall me in life – no disgrace, no calamity, (leaving me my eyes), which nature cannot repair.

Ralph Waldo Emerson

Do you imagine the universe is agitated?
Go into the desert at night and look out
at the stars... The superior person settles
her mind as the universe settles the stars
in the sky. By connecting her mind with the
subtle origin, she calms it. Once calmed, it
naturally expands, and ultimately her mind
becomes as vast and immeasurable as
the night sky.

Lao Tzu

Ne'er saw I, never felt, a calm so deep!
The river glideth at his own sweet will:
Dear God! the very houses seem asleep;
And all that mighty heart is lying still!

William Wordsworth

Clouds come floating into my life, no longer to carry rain or usher storm, but to add colour to my sunset sky.

Rabindranath Tagore

Nature does not hurry,
yet everything is accomplished.

Lao Tzu

The eternal stars shine out again,
so soon as it is dark enough.

Thomas Carlyle

This is the river... Like all profound mysteries, it is so simple that it frightens me. It wells from the rock, and flows away. For unnumbered years it has welled from the rock, and flowed away. It does nothing, absolutely nothing, but be itself.

Nan Shepherd

What moments divine,
what rapture serene.

Cole Porter

Like the musician, the painter, the poet,
and the rest, the true lover of flowers
is born, not made. And he is born to
happiness in this vale of tears, to a certain
amount of the purest joy that earth can
giver her children, joy that is tranquil,
innocent, uplifting, unfailing.

Celia Thaxter

Where hast thou wandered,
gentle gale, to find the perfumes thou
dost bring?

William Cullen Bryant

The deeper the blue becomes, the more strongly it calls man towards the infinite, awakening in him a desire for the pure and, finally, for the supernatural. The brighter it becomes, the more it loses its sound, until it turns into silent stillness and becomes white.

Wassily Kandinsky

I am sick of Portraits and wish very much to take up my Viol da Gamba and walk off to some sweet village when I can paint landskips and enjoy the fag end of life in quietness and ease.

Thomas Gainsborough

The sublime produces a beautiful calmness in the soul, which, entirely possessed by it, feels as great as it ever can feel.

Johann Wolfgang von Goethe

How sweet to be a cloud

Floating in the blue.

A. A. Milne

Every moment, the sunlight is
totally empty and totally full.

Rumi

Water, when it is still... is perfectly level and from this the carpenter takes his level. If water stilled offers such clarity, imagine what pure spirit offers! The sage's heart is stilled! Heaven and Earth are reflected in it, the mirror of all life. Empty, still, calm, plain, quiet, silent, non-active, this is the centeredness of Heaven and Earth.

Zhuangzi

I climb up, go down again, then climb up once more; between all my studies, as a relaxation I explore every footpath, always curious to see something new.

Claude Monet

Look abroad through Nature's range,

Nature's mighty law is change.

Robert Burns

In the mountain, stillness surges up to explore its own height

In the lake, movement stands still to contemplate its own depth.

Rabindranath Tagore

When the sun sets on Iona
the rocks remember the days when
they were lava.

Ailidh Lennon

It is a great art to saunter.

Henry David Thoreau

Often the mountain gives itself most completely when I have no destination, when I reach nowhere in particular, but have gone out merely to be with the mountain as one visits a friend with no intention but to be with him.

Nan Shepherd

The goal of life
is to make your heartbeat
match the beat of the universe,
to match your nature with Nature.

Joseph Campbell

How sweet the moonlight
sleeps upon this bank!

Here will we sit and let the
sounds of music

Creep in our ears; soft stillness
and the night

Become the touches of
sweet harmony.

William Shakespeare

CHAPTER
5

THE PATH TO WISDOM

Calming the mind is partly a physical process – taking deep breaths, grounding yourself by focusing on your senses – but there is also something meaningful at work.

Tranquillity comes through the nurturing of insight and spiritual growth: wisdom emerges from a calm mind, and a calm mind emerges from wisdom.

Serenity is the last lesson of culture; it is the flowering of life, the fruitage of the soul. It is precious as wisdom, more to be desired than gold... How insignificant mere money-seeking looks in comparison with a serene life – a life that dwells in the ocean of Truth, beneath the waves, beyond the reach of tempests, in the Eternal Calm!

James Allen

Do not take life too seriously
– you will never get out of it alive.

Elbert Hubbard

Perhaps time's definition
of coal is the diamond.

Kahlil Gibran

Calmness is
the cradle of power.

Josiah Gilbert Holland

Serenely full, the epicure would say,
Fate cannot harm me, I have dined to-day.

Sydney Smith

To the eyes of a miser a guinea is far more beautiful than the Sun, and a bag worn with the use of money has more beautiful proportions than a vine filled with grapes. The tree which moves some to tears of joy is in the eyes of others only a green thing which stands in the way. As a man is, so he sees.

William Blake

You are the sky.
Everything else is just the weather.

Pema Chodron

It is not the clear-sighted
who lead the world. Great
achievements are accomplished
in a blessed, warm, mental fog.

Joseph Conrad

A flower is not a flower. It is made only of non-flower elements – sunshine, clouds, time, space, earth, minerals, gardeners and so on. A true flower contains the whole universe. If we return any one of these non-flower elements to its source, there will be no flower.

Thích Nhất Hạnh

It matters not the name, the land;
my joy in all the gods abides: Even
in the cricket in the grass some
dimness of me smiles and hides.

George William Russell

The world is hard and cruel.
We are here none knows why, and
we go none knows whither.
We must be very humble.
We must see the beauty of
quietness. We must go through
life so inconspicuously that
Fate does not notice us.

And let us seek the love of
simple, ignorant people.
Their ignorance is better than all
our knowledge. Let us be silent,
content in our little corner, meek
and gentle like them.
That is the wisdom of life.

W. Somerset Maugham

It's a good idea always to do something relaxing prior to making an important decision in your life.

Paulo Coelho

Our minds need relaxation,
and give way

Unless we mix with
work a little play.

Molière

Our minds must have relaxation:
rested, they will rise up better and keener.
Just as we must not force fertile fields
(for uninterrupted production will quickly
exhaust them), so continual labour will
break the power of our minds. They will
recover their strength, however, after they
have had a little freedom and relaxation.

Seneca the Younger

The moderation of fortunate people comes from the calm which good fortune gives to their tempers.

François de La Rochefoucauld

The nearer a man comes
to a calm mind, the closer he is
to strength.

Marcus Aurelius

Man can learn nothing unless he proceeds
from the known to the unknown.

Claude Bernard

There is no such thing as an empty space or an empty time. There is always something to see, something to hear. In fact, try as we may to make a silence, we cannot.

John Cage

Constantly wrestle with your
thought, and whenever it
wanders call it back to you.

Johannes Climacus

Mirth is like a flash of lightning, that breaks through a gloom of clouds, and glitters for a moment; cheerfulness keeps up a kind of daylight in the mind, and fills it with a steady and perpetual serenity.

Joseph Addison

The more sand has escaped from the hour-glass of our life, the clearer we should see through it.

Johann Paul Friedrich Richter

There is more to life
than simply increasing its speed.

Mahatma Gandhi

We live as though there aren't enough hours in the day but if we do each thing calmly and carefully we will get it done quicker and with much less stress.

Viggo Mortensen

In Varenka, she realized that one has but to forget oneself and love others, and one will be calm, happy and noble.

Leo Tolstoy

On every mountain height
is rest.

Johann Wolfgang von Goethe

Still, there is a calm, pure harmony, and
music inside of me.

Vincent van Gogh

But once I had set out,
I was already far on my way.

Colette

CHAPTER
6

FINDING BALANCE AND CONTENTMENT

In the pursuit of serenity, balance is key: a calm state of mind comes from being able to embrace the present moment.

While there's a simplicity to this notion that's certainly easier said than done, that simplicity is also the goal: ultimately, to be content with where you are is to be at peace.

Always expecting this and expecting that. May I recommend serenity to you? A life that is burdened with expectations is a heavy life. Its fruit is sorrow and disappointment. Learn to be one with the joy of the moment.

Douglas Adams

I should say that happiness is being where one is and not wanting to be anywhere else.

Michael Frayn

This moment is fine.

Naval Ravikant

'Enough' is a feast.

Buddhist proverb

What sweet delight
a quiet life affords.

William Drummond of Hawthornden

A happy life must be to a great extent a quiet life, for it is only in an atmosphere of quiet that true joy dare live.

Bertrand Russell

Take rest; a field that has rested
gives a bountiful crop.

Ovid

He looked at an empty clock but put it back down. I picked it up and took it home. A clock without hands works fine for me. You don't see time passing.

Agnès Varda

All relaxation does is allow the truth to be felt. The mind is cleared, like a dirty window wiped clean, and the magnitude of what we might ordinarily take for granted inspires tears.

Jay Michaelson

Insight comes at a moment
of transition between work
and relaxation.

Rollo May

The earth has its music
for those who will listen.

Reginald Vincent Holmes

Relaxation means releasing all concern
and tension and letting the natural order
of life flow through one's being.

Donald Curtis

The love of learning, the
sequestered nooks, And all the
sweet serenity of books.

Henry Wadsworth Longfellow

Ragtime... but when the wearied
Band Swoons to a waltz,
I take her hand, And there we sit in
peaceful calm, Quietly sweating
palm to palm.

Aldous Huxley

My life is slipping away and I can feel it, and I should, I'm 75. I'm near the end but it doesn't frighten me. It's an adventure, and it's quite interesting to see myself slipping away. Bits slip off and leave me. Talents leave and attributes leave. I don't have the balance I used to have; I don't have the energy I used to have; I can't hear the way I used to hear; I can't see as good as I used to. I can't remember the way I used to remember.

I can't work my left hand on the banjo. It's as if I'm being prepared for something, some other adventure which is over the hill. I've got all this stuff to lose first, and then I'll be on the shadowy side of the hill, doing the next episode in the spirit world. There's still time to go yet. There's still places to go, new friends to make, maybe new songs to write and sing and jokes to tell.

Billy Connolly

If nature as a whole is good,
then pain and death are also good.

J. Baird Callicott

When you realize how perfect
everything is, you will tilt your head back
and laugh at the sky.

Buddha

As we shed our baggage,
life becomes lighter until it simply
floats away.

Christopher Fowler

Don't let your struggle become
your identity

Ralston Bowles

To contemplate is to look at shadows.

Victor Hugo

Music alone with sudden
charms can bind

The wand'ring sense, and
calm the troubled mind.

William Congreve

It is the same with people as it is with riding a bike. Only when moving can one comfortably maintain one's balance.

Albert Einstein

As you cannot have a sweet and wholesome abode unless you admit the air and sunshine freely into your rooms, so a strong body and a bright, happy, or serene countenance can only result from the free admittance into the mind of thoughts of joy and good will and serenity.

James Allen

Tranquil pleasures last the longest.
We are not fitted to bear long the burden
of great joys.

Christian Nestell Bovée

There is a calmness to a life lived in gratitude, a quiet joy.

Ralph H. Blum

The act of typing is a happy, comfortable thing for me. My fingers feel at home on a keyboard, left hand resting atop a–s–d–f, right hand on j–k–l–semicolon. I like the cursor blinking, the coffee drinking, the sitting thinking.

Amy Krouse Rosenthal

What I dream of is an art of balance, of purity and serenity devoid of troubling or depressing subject matter... a soothing, calming influence on the mind, rather like a good armchair which provides relaxation from physical fatigue.

Henri Matisse

I swim in a shaft of light, upside down, and I can see myself clearly, through and through, from every angle. Perhaps I stand on the brink of a great discovery.

Jamaica Kincaid